FACES OF PAPUA NEW GUINEA

FACES OF PAPUA NEW GUINEA

Photographs by Phil Birnbaum

Text by Andrew J. Strathern

To Bev

Faces of Papua New Guinea

First published in Australia in 1990 by
Emperor Publishing
20 Pelican Street
Darlinghurst, NSW, Australia 2010
Ph: (02) 261 4055
Fax: (02) 264 9435

National Library of Australia
Cataloguing in Publication data

Birnbaum, Phil, 1932-   .
   Faces of Papua New Guinea

   ISBN 0 7316 9762 6.

   1. Ethnology — Papua New Guinea — Pictorial
   works. I. Strathern, Andrew J., 1939-   .
   II. Title.

305.89912

Designed by Brash Design, Sydney
Edited by Sarah Overton
Map by Alistair Barnard
Typeset by Savage Type, Brisbane
Printed by Singapore National Printers Ltd
Photographic Developing and Printing by Warren Macris

CONTENTS

INTRODUCTION

Land of the bird of paradise, of seven hundred different languages, and colourful tribesmen: Papua New Guinea has certainly acquired a definite stereotype in popular magazine literature around the world. And the stereotype is not entirely inaccurate, although in certain respects it is incomplete and misleading.

It is important to remember, to begin with, that the country is only one half of the larger land mass of New Guinea, the eastern part of which, Irian Jaya, is now a province of Indonesia. Yet the two cultures are very similar.

Secondly, Papua New Guinea is now a highly successful modern democracy with a parliament based firmly on the Westminster model and an economy consisting of cash crops for export and large scale mining ventures. It is indeed a land of contrasts, in which old and new cultural styles coexist, sometimes uneasily, sometimes happily.

Papua New Guinea has a population of about 3.5 million people, with the heaviest concentrations being in the five Highland provinces: Enga, Western Highlands, Southern Highlands, Simbu, and Eastern Highlands. Its coastal dwellers are mostly speakers of Central and South Pacific languages with an economy based on fishing and trading for foodstuffs and valuables. Those dwelling inland speak a totally different group of languages. In the Highlands, cultures are based on warriorhood and wealth created by a high production of sweet potatoes and pigs. These cultures were developed over many thousands of years before the white foreigners arrived.

The earliest settlement of Papua New Guinea was probably more than thirty thousand years ago and horticulture began in the Highlands perhaps as long as nine thousand years ago. The practice of exchanging wealth goods as a means of making peaceful alliances and facilitating social intercourse has been in existence across the many ethnic and linguistic divisions for centuries. A centralized political force was less developed, but in its place was the wide array of conventions and mechanisms that groups and individuals used to conduct their exchanges, whether of yams, as in parts of the Sepik, special shell ornaments as in the islands, or pigs as in the Highlands.

Coastal societies belonging to the Austronesian tradition often do have hereditary chieftainship but in the Highlands men more often become leaders through prowess in warfare or through their ability to amass and disburse wealth. In either case, there is usually reliance on female labour, and wealthy men marry several wives as one means of securing such labour for their households.

Customs of this kind as well as the occasional practices of headhunting and cannibalism came under attack from missionaries and the colonial administrations. Fortunately, despite such efforts, much of the traditional culture still survives, and this is particularly true in the sphere of self-decoration. Some missionaries in the past did attack the practice of self-adornment, arguing that it signified sexual licentiousness inconsistent with Christian principles. However, they have now been forced to modify their stance, because of the support given by the national government to retaining traditional culture and costumes.

Papua New Guinea gained its independence from Australia on 16 September 1975. Originally the northern half (New Guinea) had been German and the southern (Papua) British, but after the Second World War the two parts were administered by Australia. At independence the two parts were finally merged together as a single country.

During the 1970s a second formal level of government was created, with provincial assemblies for each of the nineteen provinces in the country. Each assembly has its ruling group, with a premier and ministers in power. The national government allocates funds to each provincial government for its activities, and public servants are largely concerned with provincial functions.

Papua New Guinea's tribes are thus governed by a complex structure of officials and elected representatives with everyone to some extent being involved in the cash economy. Traditional cultural activities also have their role in the cash economy. In the Highlands, for example, large amounts of money are actually given away at tribal dances when one clan entertains another. The items of decoration may also cost money to hire or buy for the occasion, thereby interweaving the cash economy with traditional cultural activities.

The Papua New Guinea government has always been aware of the special character of the country's indigenous cultures and thus many of Papua New Guinea's marvellously vibrant traditions remain alive today and others have been recently revived. The Ministry for Culture and Tourism actively promotes knowledge and appreciation of local cultures and also encourages their documentation by the National Museum and the Institute of Papua New Guinea Studies.

Dances are performed at cultural shows organized on a regional basis in places such as Port Moresby, Lae, Mt. Hagen and Goroka. Dancing groups travel to these shows ('Sing Sings') and compete for prizes watched by large audiences. While they cannot reproduce the full context of local events, these dances do illustrate the spectacular aesthetics of tribal costume.

Self-decoration is both important and prominent throughout Papua New Guinea, but to divide the country by area into particular decorative styles is not possible. The most we can say is that languages and districts seem to display their own styles in a recognizable way. For certain regions a particular style element is notable: for example, human hair wigs are worn, in various forms, in the Highlands from mid-Wahgi through to Enga. Face painting is often distinctive: the bright yellow, sun-like paint work by Huli men, or the asymmetrical picking out of the eye by the Trobrianders of Milne Bay Province.

Women's decorations always differ from men's and in some places it is only the men who decorate. Yet this is not true for Mt. Hagen, nor for the coastal Papuan cultures, in which tableaux of dancers of both sexes and all ages are sometimes used to represent a whole community.

In certain coastal areas, for example, Kiwai in Western Province, dances are highly organized historical enactments. And in some places, as in Siassi, Morobe Province, the people have made a livelihood out of inventing and spreading decorations and dances to neighbouring areas in return for wealth goods. Some dances such as the Female Spirit Dance in Mt. Hagen are sacred and performed only for cults, but occasionally, these sacred dances are 'revived' for public performances.

The items used for decoration are either available in the area or obtained through the trading network of the dancers: ochres and clays for face paint; orchids and other fibres; canes, grasses, crotons, leaves, aromatic plants (favoured particularly by coastal people), and flowers; seeds, especially Job's tears; pigs' tusks, and, most important of all, various types of shell (pearl, baler, green-snail, cowrie, egg cowrie, dog-whelk) and a profusion of bird plumes, notably those of the birds of paradise (Princess Stephanie, Epimachus, King of Saxony, Superb, Prince Rudolph, Raggiana and Lesser), as well as cockatoo, eagle, parrot, and many others. The natural world is thus literally appropriated for cultural service.

There are often magical ideas associated with decoration: the dancer acquires the magnificence of the bird and like a bird is lifted into the realm of the spirits. However, the predominant motivation is the dancers' desire for colour, movement, dazzle, grace, and sensual appeal. In addition, there is the representation of the grotesque or odd which we see in Eastern Highlands masks or in the Sepik with its endless repertoire of spirit masks.

Modern items are also incorporated into the multitude of objects worn. While proud of their own pieces, Papua New Guineans will put these new items into their costumes when they have to substitute for an old item which is scarce. Beads have proved particularly popular because of their bright colours. Strings are worn as necklaces and in the Highlands smaller beads are sewn onto backings to make arm and forehead bands. Early photos of the Highlanders show them wearing fish-tin lids and labels on their hairpieces simply because of their brightness. In this way they illustrate the flexibility and adaptiveness which has enabled them to cope with the growing pressures of contemporary life.

The magnificent selection of photographs in this book demonstrates the wide range of detail in facial decoration and costume which has developed over centuries in the different cultural regions of Papua New Guinea. The photographs were taken over a period of seven years and have been carefully chosen to illustrate the distinctive patterns of decoration in tribal cultures.

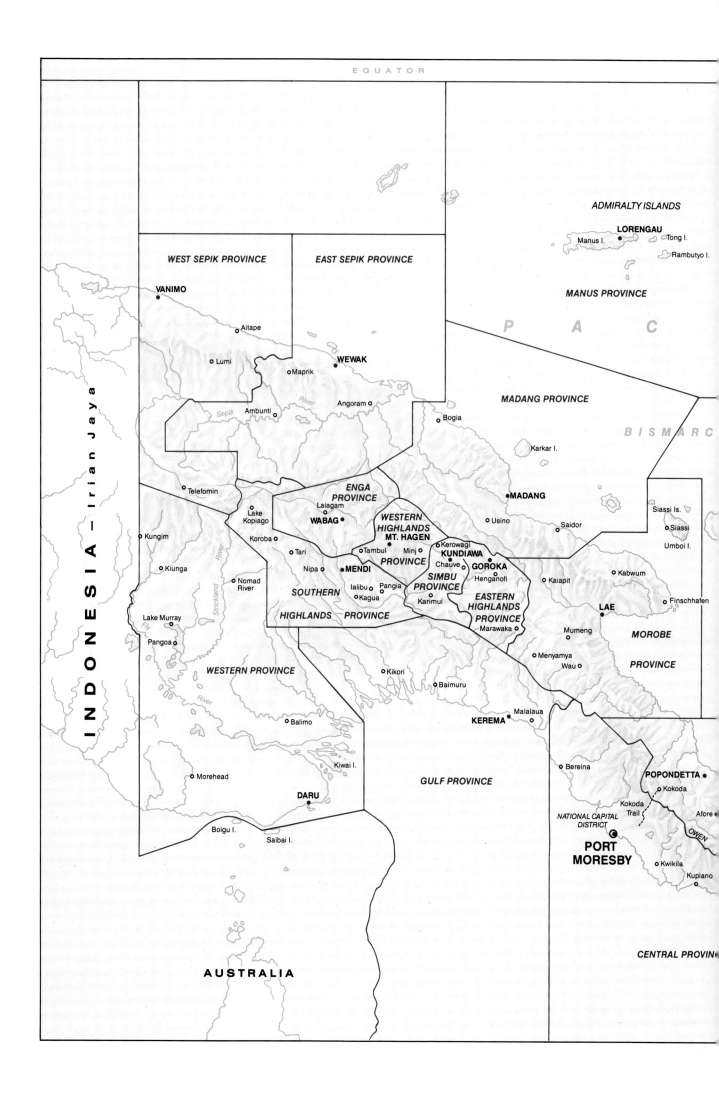

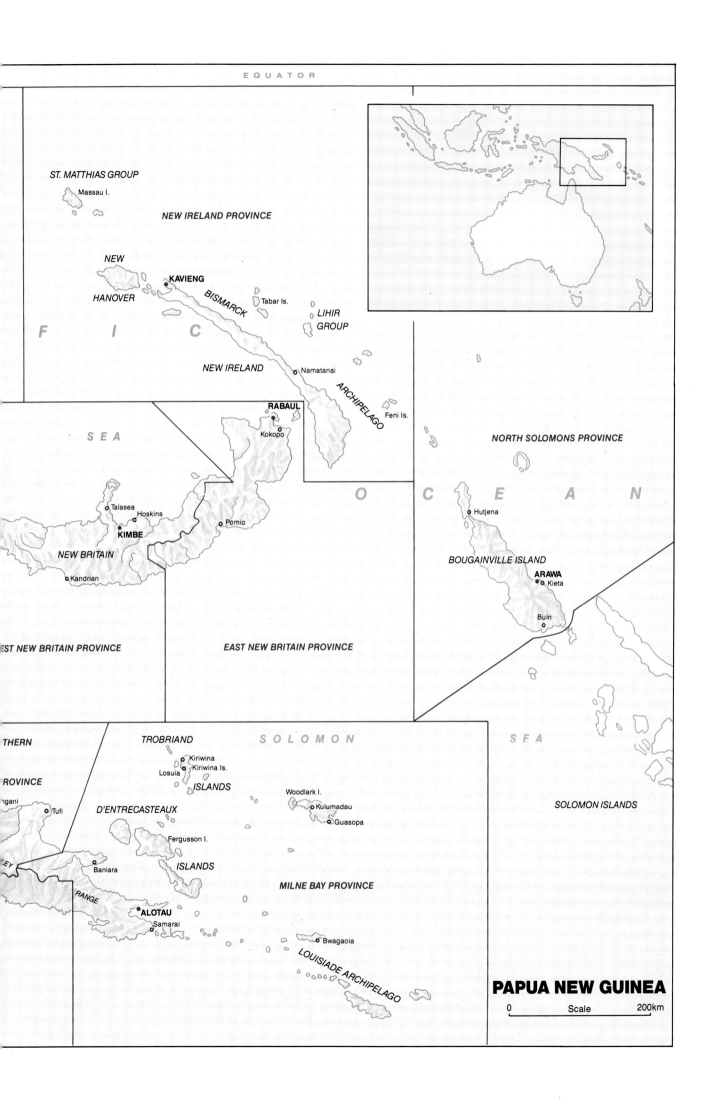

EQUATOR

ST. MATTHIAS GROUP

Massau I.

NEW IRELAND PROVINCE

NEW

HANOVER

KAVIENG

BISMARCK

Tabar Is.

LIHIR
GROUP

F I C

NEW IRELAND

Namatanai

ARCHIPELAGO

Feni Is.

RABAUL

Kokopo

S E A

NORTH SOLOMONS PROVINCE

O C E A N

Talasea

Hoskins

KIMBE

Pomio

Hutjena

NEW BRITAIN

BOUGAINVILLE ISLAND

Kandrian

ARAWA
Kieta

Buin

EST NEW BRITAIN PROVINCE

EAST NEW BRITAIN PROVINCE

S E A

THERN

TROBRIAND

S O L O M O N

ROVINCE

Kiriwina

ngani

Tufi

Losuia

Kiriwina Is.

ISLANDS

SOLOMON ISLANDS

D'ENTRECASTEAUX

Woodlark I.

Kulumadau

Guasopa

Fergusson I.

EY

Baniara

ISLANDS

MILNE BAY PROVINCE

RANGE

ALOTAU

Samarai

Bwagaoia

LOUISIADE ARCHIPELAGO

PAPUA NEW GUINEA

0   Scale   200km

THE COASTAL REGION

THE coastal region consists of the provinces of Madang, Morobe and Oro on the north coast, Milne Bay, Central, Gulf and Western on the south coast and the islands of Manus, New Britain, New Ireland and North Solomons. The population is approximately 1.8 million scattered over 320,000 square kilometres.

The dance styles of the coastal peoples from Madang and Morobe are very similar. The Siassi people, famous for their songs and dances, traded widely along the coast into Madang, distributing clay pots among other items. Oro province is the home of the Tufi and Binandere peoples (Orokaiva). Both of these peoples have distinctive dance styles with flowing feather headdresses and ordered, almost mathematical movements.

Milne Bay is best known as the home of the Trobriand Islanders. These people trace their descent through the mother rather than the father, and have an elaborate form of chieftainship which is supported by tributary gifts of the staple crop of yams. The Trobrianders are known for their lively, spirited dances.

In Central Province the Motu and Mekeo peoples are the most prominent, and both are known for their stately dance styles. These people also have chiefly systems, but descent is traced patrilineally. The Motu formerly engaged in trade with the Gulf people, travelling west by canoe to exchange sago for their pots. However, since the introduction of European utensils and foodstuffs, this trading network has declined.

In Gulf Province are the Toaripi. These traditionally fierce warriors live in the hinterland north of Kerema. In Western Province the Kiwai perform elaborate dances with mime and song, recounting folktale and history. Also in Western Province the Gogodalas, once denounced by the Protestant missionaries, have now achieved fame for their revival of dances and carvings.

The North Solomons people form a distinct physical type and are related to the Solomon Islanders who live to their south. Many of them trace descent matrilineally, as in New Britain and New Ireland, and women can be significant landholders. North Solomons was the first province to press for its separate provincial government and continues to be a focus of secessionist movements. This is partly due to feelings of shared ethnicity but also because of the presence of the large Bougainville copper mine from which they feel they should get a more substantial share of the profits.

The Manus people, like the Trobianders, are known for their spirited dances participated in by both sexes. They often have an underlying theme of eroticism. New Britain is the home of the Tolai, famous for their Tubuan spirit representations, and the Baining people, who have a firewalking ceremony as one of their rituals. In New Ireland intricate malanggan carvings are made, representing ancestors and associated creatures. Dances and feasting accompany the public unveiling of these carvings.

A dancer rests cradling his kundu drum. He has a pendant of boar's tusks and cowrie shells and a headdress of cassowary feathers secured by a barkcloth headband. (*Madang Province*)

A pensive woman from north of Popondetta has a wig of black wool, a shawl-like breast covering of beads, boar's tusks, and red and yellow crotons in her armbands. (*Northern Province*)

This man's face has been charcoaled with the outline of a beard. Cordylines, crotons and shredded banana leaves adorn his upper body. His drum has a lizard-skin top onto which beeswax has been rubbed to adjust the instrument's tone. (*Madang Province*)

16

Both these men are from Wampar, near Lae, in the Markham Valley. One is wearing a barkcloth hat and belt into which bundles of yellow-green crotons have been inserted. On his chest is a double boar's tusk pendant. The boar's tusk in the other's mouth is used to intimidate enemies. His body and face are partially smeared with clay. (*Morobe Province*)

Above: Dog's teeth sewn onto a netbag and worn as a headband form the basis of this man's individual costume. His drum is richly incised with red and white colours.

Opposite: This dancer has applied whitish clay, as well as charcoal, to his face and body. A circlet of croton leaves is on his chest and cockatoo feathers decorate his hair. (*Madang Province*)

Above: In this headdress, the dolphin, seagull and shark motifs are surmounted by an elaborate circle of downy feathers and woven fibres.

Opposite: This youth from Karkar Island wears an elaborate head assemblage with carved softwood representations of a canoe, seagull and dolphin, set off by cockatoo feathers. (*Madang Province*)

Above: This villager from Hengali, near Lae, has orange and white clay decorating her skin and a conical headdress of downy feathers.

Opposite: A dancer from Finschafen, festooned with croton leaves and long fibrous grasses, has his face stippled with yellow ochre. (*Morobe Province*)

Above: These two women have bleached reed skirts and cassowary feathers in their headdresses.

Opposite: Sweet potato leaves and orange clay covering this Wampar man's face give it a mask-like quality. (*Morobe Province*)

Above: A Finschafen man with drapings of edible hibiscus leaves over his shoulders and a mixture of leaves ringing his face.

Opposite: These Finschafen girls are wearing brightly dyed grass skirts and neck decorations of dried leaves and large betel nuts. The latter are important in coastal areas as gifts to welcome visitors to a feast or as indications of sexual interest. (*Morobe Province*)

Above left: This nassa shell mask is topped by dog's teeth on barkcloth and cropped cassowary feathers.

Above right: This mask is a modern variant being filled with strips of bright blue wool.

Opposite: Nassa shells have been sewn onto rope backings to construct this face mask. He also has a pair of boar's tusks set with resin into a collection of cowrie shells on his chest, and a cape and apron of barkcloth. (*Morobe Province*)

From Tufi, both these men are resplendent in a rainbow array of spiky parrot, cockatoo, and Raggiana bird of paradise plumes. One has extensive blazons of shell, bead and plastic jewellery on his chest, and croton leaves in his armbands. The other wears an apron, belt, armbands and wristbands of bright artificial fibres, as well as a length of the traditional barkcloth for which his province is well known. (*Northern Province*)

Above: The inverted bailer shell is very popular and with it this woman has a tuft of marsupial fur. Her headdress includes barkcloth and above this green scarab beetles encased in orchid fibre with shredded feathers on top.

Opposite: This young Popondetta girl is brightly decorated in the manner of her elders. (*Northern Province*)

Above: These women have colourful decoration on their backs including barkcloth, crimped cordyline leaves and large woven netbags.

Opposite: A young coastal dancer blowing a conch shell. This shell is used as a rhythm instrument to accompany the dancers. (*Morobe Province*)

This dancing group represents the suffering of those struck by leprosy. Their poverty is illustrated by the rags they wear and insects are kept off their sores by the constant waving of leaves. (*Madang Province*)

THE HIGHLANDS

THE Highlands region is the most populous in Papua New Guinea with approximately 1,290,000 people in a land area of 65,000 square kilometres. The peoples of this region speak languages belonging to a single large stock. They are non-Austronesians, and represent the first wave of humans to enter the island of New Guinea.

Throughout the Highlands, with its montane valleys and steep-sided ranges over 4000 metres high, the staple crop is the sweet potato, a tuber which some three to four hundred years ago probably replaced the taro and banana. Sweet potato also enabled large herds of domestic pigs to be kept, giving rise to the 'pig complex' in which the pig is a means of achieving economic, political, and ritual power.

Hunter-gatherer populations exploited the high forests and wooded valleys of the Highlands as long as thirty thousand years ago. Horticulture began in the swampy Wahgi valley (between Kundiawa and Mt. Hagen) about nine thousand years ago, as evidenced by the deep drainage ditches dug in peaty soil. Other parts may have remained largely uncultivated until the relatively late arrival of the sweet potato. This spread rapidly and widely to higher altitudes, progressively cutting back the forests, creating grazing areas for pigs, and giving access to the birds of paradise which continue to be so important for self-decoration. The older crops, such as taro, bananas and sugar cane, are now only cultivated as luxuries.

The Highlands remained unexplored by outsiders until the 1930s. The Eastern and Western Highlands, and Simbu and Enga Provinces were discovered by the Leahy Brothers and J. L. Taylor in 1933, who were travelling on foot in search of gold. The Southern Highlands were first entered also by the Leahys in 1934, and by Jack Hides and Jim O'Malley in 1935.

Exploration and settlement by Europeans was made possible by the use of small aircraft, and landing strips for these represented the first step towards establishing government influence. The Highlanders proved to be surprisingly amenable to government direction and enthusiastically set about road construction under the Australian 'Kiaps' or patrol officers. The Highlands Highway now links the whole region to the port of Lae on the northern coast. The main towns of the Highlands are Goroka, Kundiawa, Mt. Hagen and Mendi.

The Eastern Highlands is home to many small language groups. The people, in their dances, preserve the custom of wearing tall, mast-like extensions to their headdresses. This is also found in Madang and Morobe Provinces. The Bena-Bena, Anga, and Gahuku-Gama are peoples well-known in ethnographic literature. The Eastern Highlanders traditionally held initiation rituals for both sexes, but, like elsewhere, these practices have now ceased due to government and mission pressure. The Eastern Highlanders were the first to grow coffee for the purpose of earning cash.

West of the Daulo Pass (west of Goroka) the language groups increase markedly in size. Most people in Simbu Province speak dialects of the same language, and in Western Highlands all the languages belong to a single family, dominated by the Hagen and Wahgi peoples. The same is true for Enga, which contains over 100,000 speakers of a single language and dialect complex. In the Southern Highlands there are two main language groups, the first around Mendi and the other around Tari.

The Southern Highlands seems to have a greater diversity of peoples than Western Highlands or Enga. In the high density areas are peoples with recognizably Highlands-style institutions, but on the southern and western fringes of this huge province other patterns appear: tiny language groups of a few hundred or a few thousand at most, living in large, communal longhouses and sometimes harvesting sago as well as other crops. These fringe peoples show genetic similarities to the Papuans who live to their south. In the far west, beyond the huge gold mine at Porgera, live the Duna people, who form a bridge with the Ok populations across the Strickland to their west. Traditionally these people wear the most elaborate human hair horned wigs found in the whole of the Highlands. Duna music is also complex, with harmonic variations sung by small choirs of males.

From the Anga people in the east to the Duna in the far west the Highlands people exhibit a continuous intergradation and change of languages and cultural traits while still belonging to a single linguistic and perhaps ethnic stock.

One of the chief institutions found in all of these areas is the pig-killing festival, held periodically at intervals of five to ten years. These are complex occasions at which a number of debts and credits are established between networks of people. Above all they are times of heightened social activity and political display.

It is events like these which show why such tremendous emphasis is placed on self-decoration: the beautification and justification of the self for both spectators and partners.

Above: This mid-Wahgi woman wears parrot feathers, pearl shell and marsupial fur. Her armbands are woven from fibre, cane and plastic and she has a many-stranded rope belt. (*Western Highlands Province*)

Opposite: A man from Mendi holding a large pearl shell. He has a bailer on his chest and his body and face are brightly decorated with red and yellow ochre. (*Southern Highlands Province*)

Above: This mid-Wahgi woman has a scarab beetle and orchid fibre headband, with an inverted pearl shell on her neck and rubberbands on her wrists.

Opposite: The mid-Wahgi man has a headdress of Princess Stephanie tail feathers and Lesser bird of paradise and red parrot plumes. (*Western Highlands Province*)

43

These women typify mourners at a funeral. Their skin is encrusted with white and orange clay and they have boar's tusk pendants. One of them is wearing a head covering of cane inflorescence. (*Eastern Highlands Province*)

Above: A group of warriors with decoration and face-painting designed to intimidate enemies.

Opposite: This Sina Sina woman has a necklace of cassowary feathers and coix seeds (Job's tears). Her facial and body makeup indicate that she is in mourning and her weapons symbolize a desire for revenge. (*Simbu Province*)

Above: This dancer wears a chest belt of coix seeds and a headband of tree-kangaroo fur. The shape of her drum indicates coastal influence.

Opposite: This singer has a coix-seed forehead decoration topped with brown cassowary feathers. Her mouth is red from chewing betel nut, a coastal practice recently introduced into the Highlands. (*Simbu Province*)

Women from Yongamugl, near Chuave, with delicate face painting and small coix headbands.
(*Simbu Province*)

Above: Gumine men, from the southern part of Simbu, standing on guard.

Opposite: This warrior from Togoma Village, near Chuave, has a blackened face symbolizing aggressive power. He also has upturned slivers of pearl shell through his nose, a head fringe of dark cassowary feathers, and a cluster of pigs' tails around his neck. (*Simbu Province*)

These two dancers from Ketoraufa, near Goroka, portray an aspect of the spirit Nokondi. A typical characteristic of spirit-portrayal is exaggerated features of costume, such as these huge 'ear-muffs' and headpiece of human hair draped with moss. A painted strip of pandanus leaf adorns the man's forehead. Moss and grass are used by the woman to suggest her recent emergence from the forest. She has a cassowary quill through her nose and coix seed necklace. (*Eastern Highlands Province*)

These Asaro mudmen wear masks of whitish-grey clay — the colour of death and spirits. The masks are deliberately made grotesque in order to frighten off enemies. (*Eastern Highlands Province*)

These mudmen's raised eyebrows and open mouths indicate expressions of threat. Pig's teeth have been glued into their mouths. The youth accompanying the mudmen lacks an actual mask, but has plastered his head with mud. (*Eastern Highlands Province*)

Above left: A young Mt. Hagen man holding a palmwood spear strikes a statuesque pose. His body shines with tree oil which contrasts starkly with his charcoaled face. The feathers of two Lesser birds of paradise top his Superb crest.

Above right: This man, also from Mt. Hagen, has a yellow marsupial fur headband secured to a netted head covering with light brown cassowary feathers above it.

Opposite: Kane, of the Kawelka tribe in Mt. Hagen. His headdress includes eagle feathers and whole spitted lorikeets, as well as the black and turquoise ruff of a Superb bird of paradise. (*Western Highlands Province*)

Above: A pair of young women from Mount Bosavi on the Papuan Plateau shyly hold hands. They can be identified by their blackened foreheads, the combination of shells and seeds sewn onto their head coverings, and their ample reed skirts.

Opposite: A youth from Pangia wears a 'norombu' strip of cane pieces on his chest. This is reminiscent of the Hagen 'omak' originally worn to record the number of valuables given to exchange partners. (*Southern Highlands Province*)

Above: This Sina Sina man blows a horn traditionally used to call the villagers together or warn them of impending danger. Cassowary feathers fall over his face and a cassowary quill protrudes from his nose.

Opposite: This Kukama woman of Duma, near Kundiawa, has a striking bisected face-paint design and a wig surrounded by tree moss. Her chest decoration is made of raffia. (*Simbu Province*)

Above: Simbu women in a dance procession. Each has a necklace of a double boar's tusk and a belt made out of string shells. (*Simbu Province*)

Opposite: A Gorokan woman with a back decoration of strips of pandanus. Her extremely large earrings are made of dog's teeth. (*Eastern Highlands Province*)

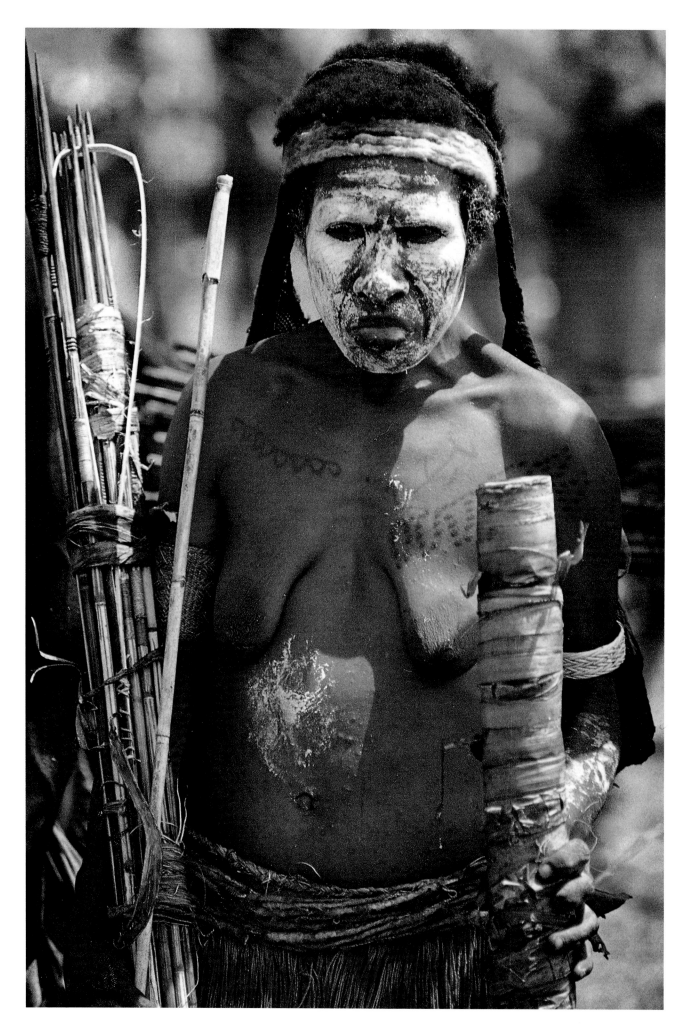

Above: White clay and white chicken feathers adorn this older woman's body and wig.

Opposite: This woman is carrying a sheaf of weapons and a container normally used for tree oil. (*Simbu Province*)

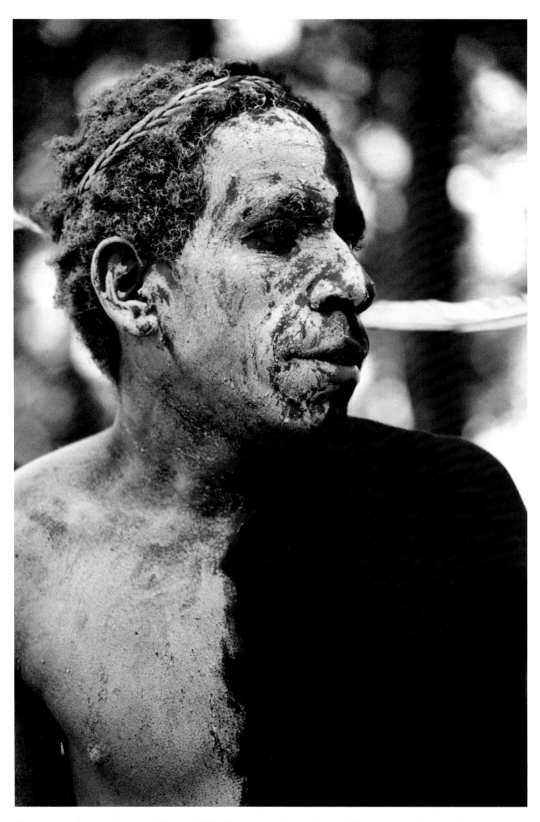

These two dancers have white and black contrasting makeup. The woman is wearing a conical wig decorated with tufts of soft chicken feathers. Pit-pit inflorescences cover her back, and she has necklaces of coix and other seeds. (*Simbu Province*)

Above: This Mendi woman is wearing a knotted netbag on her head, a beautifully shaped pearl shell on her chest, and a large necklace of cowrie shells with massive strands of black plastic beads.

Opposite: This man from the Mendi area wears a reddened headnet with cropped black cassowary feathers and a pointed bailer shell at his neck. His steel axe has 'akis' (Pidgin English for 'axe') scratched into its painted surface. White beads have been used for his forehead band to intimate the traditional nassa shells. (*Southern Highlands Province*)

These Angas of Marawaka have draped their heads and bodies with coix seeds and ragged clothing such as netbags and string aprons. They are portraying grief at a funeral. (*Eastern Highlands Province*)

Above: The blackened skin of this Anga boy contrasts sharply with the whitish-grey colour of his coix seed 'halter'.

Opposite: This young woman from Obura, near Kainantu, has her face fringed with marsupial furs, cowries, nuts and coix-seed strings. She also has a cassowary quill through her nose and two large egg cowries between her breasts. (*Eastern Highlands Province*)

A Simbu woman with a whole marsupial fur cap, cowrie necklace, and a King of Saxony crest feather in her nose. (*Simbu Province*)

A Simbu warrior with a brightly painted shield, neck shell and conus in his nose. The bailer on his forehead is topped with a cassowary feather spray and Red bird of paradise plumes. Parrots' wings cover his ears. (*Simbu Province*)

Above: These elaborate headdresses are worn by Asaro dancers. Painted designs (clan emblems) mingle with bright bird of paradise and spitted lorikeet plumes.

Opposite: Asaro man with a magnificent pair of boar's tusks through his nose. (*Eastern Highlands Province*)

Above: Bright yellow and red face decorations give a mask-like appearance to this Huli boy. He is also wearing a marsupial fur headband, pearl shell, and red and blue beads.

Opposite: Tradestore paints have replaced earth dyes for face painting in most areas. This youth has a large cassowary feather spray at the top of his wig. (*Southern Highlands Province*)

The Huli are one of the most decorative peoples of Papua New Guinea. This man has cane bands as neck circlets and bead 'pipings' around his forehead.

This initiate is being fitted with a headdress of marsupial fur and feathers above his 'manda hare' wig, as a sign that he has achieved adult status. The Superb crest on his forehead also indicates his new status.

This man's 'manda tene' (downturned) wig has a Superb bird of paradise crest in the centre. Dried flowers are arranged at the bottom.

The predominant colours for Huli 'Sing Sings' are yellow and red. The human hair wig has been dyed red and is interspersed with bird of paradise feathers. (*Southern Highlands Province*)

Above: This man's upturned 'manda hare' wig reveals 'gai gulu' (fringing) feathers. He is also wearing a hornbill beak, pig's tusks, and a finely woven belt.

Opposite: A 'manda hare' wig of human hair being made. It is shaped with long wooden pins. (*Southern Highlands Province*)

Above: The bird of paradise is the emblem of Papua New Guinea. Only nationals are permitted to shoot the birds and it can only be done with a bow and arrow. The meat is eaten and the plumage used to decorate headdresses.

Opposite: A typical example of a Huli wearing an imaginative headdress of bird of paradise feathers. His apron is made of pigs' tails. (*Southern Highlands Province*)

Contrasts in young Huli decoration. One has an imitation upturned adult wig made out of twisted canes and grasses with a cassowary head fringe. The other has a headpiece of sweet potato vines. (*Southern Highlands Province*)

Two Huli men. One has bunches of yellow everlasting daisies on his wig and a snakeskin forehead band. The other has an elongated piece of cane through his nose. Both are wearing pearl shell necklaces. (*Southern Highlands Province*)

Above: These dancers have long poles suspended on their backs, topped with Princess Stephanie feathers and red and yellow bird of paradise plumes.

Opposite: A Gorokan dancer with an elaborately decorated board which will be mounted on his back. (*Eastern Highlands Province*)

Above: This man from the upper Asaro is impersonating a wild bush spirit, with a conical bark mask and an abundance of tree moss for his hair and beard.

Opposite: A wig made of cassowary feathers and topped with a single black cockatoo feather. The man's bow is of black palm. (*Eastern Highlands Province*)

These two dancers are from the Kaike dance group. In his teeth he is holding an elaborate ornament made from nassa shells and large, mottled cowries. This acts as a threatening gesture to his enemies. She is holding a large cowrie in her mouth and wears crossover necklaces of coix seeds. (*Eastern Highlands Province*)

Opposite and above left: Villagers from Korfena, near Goroka, perform the frog dance wearing mud masks reminiscent of the Asaro mudmen. The mouth slits imitate the mouths of frogs.

Above right: This masked dancer with sharp fingers of bamboo represents a bush demon. (*Eastern Highlands Province*)

These Anga women are wearing the long barkcloth capes typical of their area. Their arrows are a reminder of their reputation as warriors. (*Eastern Highlands Province*)

The predominant decorative feature of these Anga women is short egg-cowrie necklaces, with longer strands of ordinary cowries. They also have numerous marsupial fur tassels and woven chains of grass. (*Eastern Highlands Province*)

These young men from Laiagam have just completed the bachelors' purification ritual. They have beautifully shaped wigs, a band of beads on their foreheads, King of Saxony crests bent around their charcoaled faces and black sicklebill feathers. Cassowary leg-bone spatulae protrude from their ears and they have cordyline leaves down their backs. (*Enga Province*)

Above: A Mt. Hagen man dressed for a 'mörl' dance. He has an elongated human hair wig, feather plaque and a cuscus shell in his nose. The bamboo sticks on his chest are 'omak'. They are particular to the Hagen people and mark the number of pearl shells given away in 'moka' exchanges. Note the local government councillor's badge on his wig. (*Western Highlands Province*)

Opposite: The leaves pinned to this wig and its horned shape give it a most unusual appearance. (*Enga Province*)

Above: These boys from Maramuni, near Laiagam, do not yet wear the horned wig which indicates maturity. Instead their hair is covered with beaten barkcloth and their faces are obscured by charcoal. Cassowary bone spatulae protrude from beneath their head coverings. (*Enga Province*)

Opposite: This man from the Poindoma Village, near Mendi, has a large bailer shell on his chest and a glistening mop of black cassowary feathers over his bright red head covering. This is not a traditional arrangement, just a personal choice. (*Southern Highlands Province*)

Above: Mother and daughter wearing freshly dried reed skirts. The daughter has a headdress of parrot feathers and holds a gourd for lime, which is chewed with betel nut. (*Eastern Highlands Province*)

Opposite: A large fringe of black cassowary feathers covers the eyes of this woman. She also wears a whole marsupial fur, a reversed shell at her neck and a stranded belt of woven fibres. (*Simbu Province*)

Above: His headdress is made of chicken feathers and his skin is daubed with white clay.

Opposite: This man from Bena Bena, near Goroka, has a boar's tusk pendant, scarab beetle headband, and a cane chest belt. Marsupial tails protrude from his headdress. (*Eastern Highlands Province*)

This mourning ceremony is being carried out by the Boldi people who live near Goroka. Mourning can last many months and during this period the people dress in ragged netbags and cover their skin with clay and ashes. The grave is adorned with flowers and cordylines mark its edges. (*Eastern Highlands Province*)

Above: This man from the Upper Asaro, near Goroka, has combined charcoal and oil to give his skin a gritty appearance. He has also wrapped old netbag material around his head.

Opposite: This Asaro woman has a head cape of long cordyline leaves. Suspended from the black palm pin inserted in her nose is a coix seed necklace. (*Eastern Highlands Province*)

Above: These women dancers are from Erave, near Kagua. They hold long sticks with which they symbolically strike the ground to signify their role as gardeners. Red and yellow ochre stripes adorn their bodies and they have coverings of crimped cordylines. (*Southern Highlands Province*)

Opposite: These highly decorated girls are in full dance array. Circlets of parrot feathers and flowing plumes of the Red and Lesser birds of paradise adorn their headdresses and armbands. (*Simbu Province*)

Above: These Mt. Hagen dancers are celebrating the handing over of a gift to another group. Their headnets and overall decorations show remarkable uniformity. The dance being performed is the 'mörl'.

Opposite: This Mt. Hagen man has a headdress of eagle and parrot feathers. Forest ferns tucked into his beard and armbands offset the charcoal and grease on his body. (*Western Highlands Province*)

Above: These Kawelka dancers are wearing formal plaque ('köi wal') headdresses constructed from parrot feathers and King of Saxony crests. The style of apron and shell decoration which the dancer on the right wears indicates he has come from the town of Tambul.

Opposite: This man is also from Kawelka, near Mt. Hagen. He has cassowary spatulae and Prince Rudolph bird of paradise feathers on either side of his plaque headdress. (*Western Highlands Province*)

Men from Tambul performing the 'mörl' dance. They have smartly shaped horned wigs ('peng lepa') topped with light blue Prince Rudolph feathers and cropped cassowary pom-poms. They also have bailer shells over their foreheads. (*Western Highlands Province*)

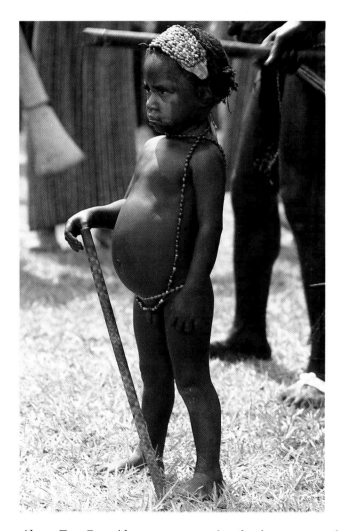 

Above: Two Bomai boys accompanying the dance group of their elders. One has a band of coix seeds on his forehead and the other has a headdress of downy chicken feathers.

Opposite: This man, also from Bomai, near Kundiawa, is completely covered in charcoal and oil signifying his status as a warrior. (*Simbu Province*)

These Bomai dancers have matted headdresses decorated with cassowary feathers. The tradestore whistle is used as a rhythm instrument to punctuate their dance. (*Simbu Province*)

Hewa man from the Lake Kopiago region. He has a flowing cassowary feather headdress and brown marsupial fur headband. (*Southern Highlands Province*)

Mt. Hagen man dressed for the 'mörli' (courting dance) which takes place after an exchange occasion. He and his companion have bright marsupial furs and cockatoo feather headpieces. Their headbands are of scarab beetle. (*Western Highlands Province*)

Youth wearing a netted headcap trimmed with cassowary feathers and soft strips of marsupial fur. (*Simbu Province*)

This Goroka man has brightly dyed feathers and a matching marsupial fur headband. (*Eastern Highlands Province*)

Men from Nipa. Both their headnets and front aprons are brightly coloured with earth dyes. Downy sprays of young eagle feathers top their wigs. (*Southern Highlands Province*)

Mangiro youth group called 'Tope' from Upper Asaro. They have long conical wigs made from teasel heads (burrs). (*Eastern Highlands Province*)

Two mid-Wahgi men. One is wearing a whole tree-kangaroo fur, along with Princess Stephanie plumes, parrot feathers and King of Saxony crests. The other has a double forehead band of fibre and plastic, parrot feathers beside his ear and tail plumes through his nose. (*Western Highlands Province*)

This Panga women's group from Mt. Hagen is fully decorated for its stately 'werl' dance.
The participants have 'teardrop' facial designs and headdresses of eagle feathers topped by
sicklebill. (*Western Highlands Province*)

Above: This mui pukl wal woman has a large array of coix seeds normally used for mourning, and a pearl shell slung low on her waist. The leaves used are kuklumb, not a usual part of decoration.

Opposite: Amb mui pukl wal (women with netbags full of greens). These tribal dancers humble themselves by donning poor and dark decorations and bowing their heads. They are, in fact, conveying a boast that their husbands' group is rich and powerful. (*Western Highlands Province*)

These young Maring men from north of Mt. Hagen are wearing 'mamp gunc' wigs and headdresses of eagle and cockatoo feathers. They are performing a dance after seclusion. The wigs are elaborately constructed on frames using resin, and the initiates' hair is pulled into the frames. Green scarab beetle beads cover the surface. The wigs indicate that the youths' kinsmen have killed enemies in battle. (*Western Highlands Province*)

THE SEPIK

THE Sepik region comprises the East and West Sepik Provinces and stretches to the border with Irian Jaya. It has a population of approximately 400,000 tribal people and a land area of 80,000 square kilometres.

The East Sepik is dominated by the waters of the Sepik River. Its riverine communities are famous for the extraordinary development of their visual art forms. These are expressed in sacred carvings, cult houses and large wall paintings, as well as in flamboyant self-decoration on ritual occasions.

The West Sepik is less well known to the outside world. In its interior there are people of the Ok culture complex. These are small mountain dwelling populations with a less elaborate material culture than the Sepik River peoples, but with highly graded initiation rituals and cult temples which supposedly hold sacred power over several local areas.

The best-known cultures in the East Sepik are those found in the middle Sepik area, including the Abelam, Iatmul, Arapesh, and Boiken. The Iatmul and Arapesh were originally studied by the anthropologists Gregory Bateson and Margaret Mead. Mead's study of 'sex and temperament' in the Sepik was one of the earliest studies to suggest that sex roles are culturally variable. A feature of all these cultures is the 'haus tambaran', or sacred cult-house, in which initiation rituals are practised. These contain carved representations of ancestors and spirits. Among the Abelam the cult-houses have huge wall panels painted with representations of the 'Nggwalndu' spirits.

Sepik people are horticulturalists, fishermen, hunters and, in some places, sago producers. The middle Sepik cultures are largely based on the production of yams, and from this has emerged a system of competitive gift giving between exchange partners. Certain yams are cultivated for their length and size, and when harvested are decorated and given away. These competitive exchanges of yams, accompanied by much speech-making, are the equivalent in the Sepik of the pig and shell exchanges found in the Highlands.

The Sepik-Ramu floodplain, which stretches towards the northern coast, was formerly a huge inland sea. Some six thousand years ago it began to recede with the tectonic uplift of mountain ranges. More recently, the river and its inland lakes were threatened with the weed salvinia. However, by 1985 this was brought under control by the introduction of a parasitic weevil.

Sepik art has been greatly sought after by collectors and tourists since the 1890s. In addition to carvings and decorations the people manufacture fine pots and coloured netbags, for their own use as well as for sale to visitors.

Sepik costumes are quite distinct from those of the Highlands, but related to those of Morobe and Madang. Men are distinguished by the construction of elaborate face masks surrounded by shells and feathers, and women by their coloured netbags or 'bilums'.

A masked dancer with an elaborate collection of bailer shells. The boar's tusks sewn onto the netbag are representative of the 'tambaran' spirit. (*East Sepik Province*)

147

Above: This man with boar's tusks held threateningly in his mouth is portraying a bush spirit. He has a fringe of dog's teeth above his shell bead band, topped with black cassowary feathers.

Opposite: The facial designs accentuate the flow of lines around this woman's mouth and eyes. (*East Sepik Province*)

Two women from a Karawari River (tributary of the Sepik) village. They both have coloured facial ochre markings and long coix seed necklaces.

Above: This child is selling pineapples at the local market. (*West Sepik Province*)

Opposite: A Karawari woman with a multicoloured stippled face design. This type of makeup has recently become popular with young women in the Highlands. (*East Sepik Province*)

Market day. These women are selling sweet potato leaves, tomatoes, onions, paw paws and pineapples. (*West Sepik Province*)

Opposite: A man from Ok region near Telefomin pauses to smoke a homemade cigarette. His penis-gourd comes from the bottle gourd plant (*above*). (*West Sepik Province*)

Above: This man from Oksapmin, east of Telefomin, has chosen a full set of cockatoo feathers for his headdress and a feather tassel for his penis-gourd. He also has a cross-chest necklace of shells and a set of cane for his belt.

Opposite: This Oksapmin villageman has a headdress of parrot feathers supported on a wicker frame and a cockatoo feather through his nose. The circlets on his eyes give an impression of spectacles. His back is covered by cassowary feathers. (*West Sepik Province*)